U.S. Fish & Wildlife Service

I0500393

A Conceptual Approach to Evaluating Grassland Restoration Potential on Huron Wetland Management District, South Dakota

Biological Technical Publication

BTP-R6016-2012

Murray K. Laubhan[1]

Bridgette Flanders-Wanner[2, 4]

Rachel A. Laubhan[3]

[1] U.S. Fish and Wildlife Service, Region 6, Division of Biological Resources, Stafford, KS

[2] U.S. Fish and Wildlife Service, Huron Wetland Management District, Huron, SD

[3] U.S. Fish and Wildlife Service, Quivira National Wildlife Refuge, Stafford, KS

[4] Current Address: U.S. Fish and Wildlife Service, Branch of Refuge Biology, Vancouver, WA

Cover image: Waubay National Wildlife Refuge
Photo credit: Laura Hubers, USFWS

Author Contact Information:

Murray K. Laubhan
U.S. Fish and Wildlife Service, Region 6
Division of Biological Resources
1434 NE 80th Street
Stafford, KS 67578
Phone: (620) 486-2393
E-mail: Murray_Laubhan@fws.gov

Bridget Flanders-Wanner
U.S. Fish and Wildlife Service, Region 1
Branch of Refuge Biology
1211 SE Cardinal Court, Suite 100
Vancouver, WA 98683
Phone: (360) 604-2558
E-mail: Bridgette_Flanders-Wanner@fws.gov

Rachel A. Laubhan
U.S. Fish and Wildlife Service
Quivira National Wildlife Refuge
1434 NE 80th Street
Stafford, KS 67578
Phone: (620) 486-2393
E-mail: Rachel_Laubhan@fws.gov

Recommended citation:

Laubhan, M. K., B. Flanders-Wanner, and R. A. Laubhan. 2012. A conceptual approach to evaluating grassland restoration potential on Huron Wetland Management District, South Dakota. U.S. Department of Interior, Fish and Wildlife Service, Biological Technical Publication FWS/BTP-R6016-2012, Washington, D.C.

For additional copies or information, contact:

Wayne J. King
Chief, Division of Biological Resources
U.S. Fish and Wildlife Service, Region 6
P.O. Box 25486
Denver Federal Center
Denver, CO 80225-0486
Phone: (303) 236-8102
E-mail: wayne_j_king@fws.gov

Series Senior Technical Editor:

Stephanie L. Jones
Nongame Migratory Bird Coordinator
U.S. Fish and Wildlife Service, Region 6
P.O. Box 25486 DFC
Denver, Colorado 80225
Phone: (303) 236-4409
E-mail: Stephanie_Jones@fws.gov

ISSN 2160-9498 Electronic ISSN 2160-9497 Biological Technical Publications online:
http://library.fws.gov/BiologicalTechnicalPublications.html

Table of Contents

List of Figures

List of Tables

Acknowledgements

W. J. King provided funding and coordinated activities associated with this report. The staff of the Huron Wetland Management District conducted a tour of district lands, summarized existing data, and openly discussed management opportunities and constraints that should be considered in developing a conceptual management approach. Reviews of earlier drafts greatly improved the report, particularly those provided by D. Azure, P. M. Drobney, J. S. Gleason, R. A. Gleason, K. W. Kelsey, W. J. King, and C. Mowry. M. J. Artmann kindly assisted in the development of tables and figures. The findings and conclusions in this article are those of the authors and do not necessarily represent the views of the U.S. Fish and Wildlife Service.

Executive Summary

The 1997 National Wildlife Refuge System Improvement Act requires each administrative unit in the National Wildlife Refuge System to develop a Comprehensive Conservation Plan (CCP). As part of this planning process, biological goals and objectives must be developed based on the best available scientific information. To assist with the CCP process, Huron Wetland Management District (WMD) requested assistance in developing a conceptual approach for evaluating ecological restoration options of grassland tracts administered by the district. Our approach was to summarize and organize general concepts in a framework that could be used to evaluate restoration potential rather than attempt to develop management recommendations that included specific planting techniques or management strategies, although this also will be required to ensure long-term success.

We developed our approach based on a review of the literature to identify attributes that influenced the success of past ecological restoration efforts. We developed summaries of this information to provide managers and biologists with an overview of factors to consider when evaluating restoration potential. Development of clear and unambiguous goals and objectives was identified as a critical initial consideration because they define expectations, help determine strategies to be implemented, and form the foundation of meaningful monitoring programs. Consideration of scale (both spatial and temporal) and biological factors (both abiotic and biotic) also is important. Collectively, these attributes are useful for determining the causes of grassland degradation, defining the restoration potential of a site, and identifying the most appropriate remediation techniques.

We used these general concepts and attributes to develop a conceptual hierarchical framework for evaluating restoration potential of individual grassland tracts on Huron WMD, which encompasses approximately 17,790 km^2 (6,869 mi^2) in portions of eight counties in east-central South Dakota. District staff currently manages 4,644 ha (11,476 ac) of grasslands, including 2,537 ha (6,270 ac) that have never been tilled and are classified as native sod. A focus of upland management is reconstructing grasslands on previously farmed sites and restoring existing grasslands (i.e., native sod with no previous cropping history) that have been invaded by non-native grasses to more native vegetation communities.

The goal of ecological restoration on Huron WMD is to restore native grasses and forbs that provide the structure and resources necessary to support populations of target migratory birds. However, objectives had not yet been developed that identified specific, measurable targets regarding plant community composition or wildlife species. Thus, we applied our approach to a set of example objectives that included developing appropriate seed mixtures for reconstruction projects that benefit migratory birds, estimating the potential for non-native plant species establishment, and determining wildlife values that would be expected following restoration. The framework we developed incorporated attributes that could be used to assess site conditions relative to the objectives as well as interim steps that provide examples of how attribute information can be combined to facilitate evaluation. Finally, outcomes based on evaluation of the attributes are identified to provide a means to assign priorities to restoration projects.

Developing an approach for evaluating and prioritizing sites for restoration is a complex and uncertain process. Although much is known regarding factors controlling plant community establishment and the relationships between plant communities and wildlife habitat suitability, the relative importance of these factors often varies among and within sites depending on past perturbations and surrounding landscape conditions. Consequently, a structured framework can promote standardized evaluations and improve communication on site, while providing a method to systematically deconstruct complex problems and provide greater objectivity when making restoration decisions.

© Chris Bailey

Introduction

The 1997 National Wildlife Refuge System Improvement Act requires each administrative unit in the National Wildlife Refuge System to develop a Comprehensive Conservation Plan (CCP) that includes biological goals and objectives that are based on the best available scientific information. Goals are general descriptions of desired future conditions, but objectives are more specific and must be measurable, achievable, results oriented, and time specific. In many cases, objectives are habitat-based and specify the guilds of wildlife species that will benefit from attainment of each objective.

To assist with the CCP process, Huron Wetland Management District (WMD) requested that we synthesize information on ecological restoration approaches for grasslands that would help them develop goals and objectives to achieve a desired grassland condition defined as a "a mixture of native grasses and forbs that provide the structure and foods necessary to support target migratory bird species." We decided the best approach was to integrate relevant information from different scientific disciplines into a framework that could

be used to evaluate ecological restoration potential of different grassland tracts. Although some information we used is based on studies conducted outside the northern Great Plains, they were relevant to Huron WMD because they addressed ecological drivers (e.g., soils, moisture, and climate) that are primary determinants of plant germination and survival regardless of geographic location (Simpson et al. 1989, Aronson and Le Floc'h 1996, Ehrenfeld 2000).

The desired outcomes used in the document are examples developed by the authors and are not those of Huron WMD. This document is not intended to serve as a complete guide that includes post-establishment management recommendations, but as an example of the process. Consequently, on-the-ground experience in restoring sites, in combination with the literature used in the report, should be used to evaluate the relevancy of the goals, attributes used to evaluate site conditions, and desired outcomes.

Review of the Literature

Goal and Objective Setting

The rapid rise of ecological restoration has resulted in widely varying interpretations regarding what is meant by the term and what constitutes success (Palmer et al. 1997, Ruiz-Jaen and Aide 2005). Some individuals advocate that restoration is as much ethical as technical and should include historical, social, cultural, political, aesthetic, and moral aspects, as well as ecological principles (Higgs 1997). Even within a single discipline such as ecology, restoration can range from a focus on particular species to entire ecosystems (Risser 1995, Falk et al. 1996, Kershner 1997). These different approaches can result in widely varying goals and objectives. Strict definitions of restoration often have goals that refer to historic conditions and objectives that mention emulating the structure, function, diversity, and dynamics of the pre-defined ecosystem (Aronson et al. 1993). Achieving this level of success is rare because it is difficult both to determine the exact structure and function of historic ecosystems and to establish the full complement of species and range of occurrence levels historically present (Cairns 1991, Lockwood and Pimm 1999). Consequently, some practitioners have recommended evaluating restoration projects in terms of achieving functional (e.g., erosion control) or structural (e.g., species composition) goals and objectives (Whisenant 1999, Piper and Pimm 2002), whereas others advocate defining restoration categories (e.g., restoration, rehabilitation, reallocation) that have different goals and objectives (Aronson et al. 1993, Keddy 1999). In these latter scenarios, goals do not necessarily bear an intrinsic relationship with pre-disturbance ecosystem structure and function and may even consist of innovative combinations of native or introduced species (D'Antonio and Meyerson 2002).

Given this disparity, developing goals and explicit objectives is the first and most important component of a project. Clear and unambiguous goals and objectives define expectations, help determine strategies to be implemented, and form the foundation of meaningful monitoring programs. Ehrenfeld (2000) discusses some common restoration goals and objectives, the implications of each from a practical perspective, and suggests that there is no single paradigm or context for setting goals and objectives; rather, goals and objectives need to be developed for each project relative to desired outcomes (Jordan et al. 1987, Buckley 1989). In addition, goals and objectives should be established based on a realistic expectation of what restoration can accomplish. Factors to consider include extent of degradation, information available for addressing

problems, and costs (Society of Ecological Restoration 2004). Ensuring that goals are realistic often can be addressed by defining categories of restoration success such as those described by Aronson et al. (1993).

Spatial Scale

The importance of various abiotic and biotic factors in developing restoration goals and approaches can vary depending on the spatial scale considered (Aronson and Le Floc'h 1996, Goldstein 1999). Reducing or removing sources of degradation that compromise system functionality often is recommended as an initial step in ecological restoration to ensure long-term sustainability (Whisenant 1995). Identifying the source of degradation is important because the presence or absence of a plant or animal species in a specific area may be controlled by factors operating at scales much larger than the site being evaluated for management (Byre 1997, White and Walker 1997, George and Zack 2001). Understanding the extent of degradation also is critical as more human intervention often is required as degradation increases and eventually it may not be possible to completely reverse some damages. This concept, termed thresholds of environmental change, is well established in ecology (Holling 1973, Wissel 1984) and is being applied in range management (Friedel 1991, Laylock 1991) to evaluate site conditions. Failure to consider these scale-dependent factors can lead to erroneous conclusions regarding remediation techniques, the most appropriate plant species to restore, and, ultimately, the ability of restoration projects to achieve intended goals.

Temporal Scale

Natural systems, including grasslands, are extremely dynamic (Pickett and Parker 1994) and considerable evidence indicates feedback occurs between species composition and ecosystem processes. This feedback causes many ecosystem processes to develop over different time scales (Palmer et al. 1997, Kulmatiski et al. 2006). Consequently, many communities exist in perpetual states of nonequlibirium (Wiens 1984, Pickett et al. 1992) and exhibit both physical and biological variability (Horne and Schnieder 1995, Palmer and Poff 1997). Perennial plant species tend to dominate both terrestrial and aquatic systems during relatively stable periods, whereas annuals tend to predominate following shorter temporal scales. At shorter temporal scales, dramatic changes in plant composition (e.g., forb diversity) also can occur from late spring to winter in the same year.

Although dynamic conditions are difficult to describe succinctly, temporal changes in plant community composition and structure are important considerations when evaluating ecological restoration potential and developing management strategies. Successful establishment of a target plant community may require the use of certain plant species, such as nitrogen-fixing legumes in arid and semi-arid ecosystems, at specific times during the restoration process (Jenkins et al. 1987, Jarrell and Virginia 1990, Paine 1996). Long-term sustainability of a plant community also requires that sufficient plant diversity be present to persist across the full range of environmental fluctuations characteristic of the site (Schulze and Mooney 1993, Davis and Richardson 1995, Palmer et al. 1997). Adequately incorporating the temporal dynamics of ecological restoration projects may require a sequential, multi-step process or defining the "potential" of a site at different stages of succession based on climate, soils, hydrology, seed type and availability, plant competition, plant-animal interactions, and other factors (Palmer et al. 1997).

Abiotic and Biotic Factors

Although restoration goals can focus on a range of outcomes, a principle common to most restoration approaches is the need to incorporate knowledge of processes (Ehrenfeld 2000). Not only is knowledge of processes (e.g., hydrology, nutrient cycling) necessary to evaluate the full range of remediation measures available, this knowledge is also critical to evaluating outcomes (King and Hobbs 1996, Montalvo et al. 1997)

and, ultimately, to developing improved, site-specific restoration methods (Ehrenfeld 2000). However, ecological processes are complex assemblages of interacting factors and direct measurement is often not feasible. Therefore, indicators often must be used as surrogate measures to assess abiotic and biotic site conditions. Knowledge of landscape position, soil physical structure and chemistry, and climate often can be used to determine the range of soil moisture conditions occurring at a site.

The specific abiotic factors to consider when developing an approach to evaluate ecological restoration potential are best determined by the goals that have been established. A literature review documented that factors considered in different projects were diverse and tended to be individualistic (Ehrenfeld 2000). However, from a management perspective, goals alone often are not sufficient to limit the number of factors to a manageable level and additional criteria must be used to narrow the selection to those that are most relevant. Several articles addressing this subject have been published, including a list of vital ecosystem attributes (Aronson et al. 1993), information syntheses that provide general guidance (Whisenant 1995), and several practical case histories (Tongway and Ludwig 1996, Eliason and Allen 1997, Breshears et al. 2001, Sheley and Krueger-Mangold 2003, King and Hobbs 2006). A common feature of these articles is the importance placed on identifying key abiotic and biotic factors related to system structure and function in the context of stated goals.

Study Site

Huron WMD was established on May 31, 1992 under the authority of the Migratory Bird Hunting and Conservation Stamp Act (16 U.S.C. 718), which authorizes the acquisition, lease, purchase, or exchange of small wetland and pothole areas designated as Waterfowl Production Areas (WPA). Huron WMD encompasses eight counties in east-central South Dakota, an area of approximately 17,790 km^2 (6,869 mi^2) (Fig. 1). In 2000, lands administered by Huron WMD included 60 WPAs (5,807 ha [14,350 ac]), 1,425 wetland easements (27,843 ha [68,800 ac]), 147 grassland easements (22,541 ha [55,700 ac]), and 63 conservation easements (4,087 ha [10,100 ac]) (U.S. Fish and Wildlife Service 2000). Although at least one WPA is located in every county, the majority occur in Beadle, Hand, and Jerauld counties (Fig. 1).

Huron WMD currently manages 4,644 ha (11,476 ac) of grasslands, including 2,537 ha (6,270 ac) that have never been tilled and are classified as native sod (Table 1). Approximately 2,411 ha (95% [5,957 ac]) of native sod are dominated by more than 50% non-native species, whereas only 126 ha (5% [311 ac]) are dominated by more than 50% native species. The remaining 2,107 ha (45% [5,206 ac]) of grasslands are comprised of tracts that have been reseeded to native plants (713 ha [1,762 ac]) or have been subjected to some type of agricultural land-use practice (1,394 ha [3,444 ac]). Based on surveys of vegetation composition on a portion of planted native tracts, it is estimated that 521 ha (73% [1,287 ac]) are comprised of >50% native species and 192 ha (27% [475 ac]) are comprised of <50% native species (Table 1).

Huron WMD lands include both cool-season native grasses dominated by green needlegrass (*Nassella viridula*), western wheatgrass (*Pascopyrum smithii*), and porcupinegrass (*Hesperostipa spartea*) and warm-season grass dominated by big bluestem (*Andropogon gerardii*), switchgrass (*Panicum virgatum*), Indiangrass (*Sorghastrum nutans*), and little bluestem (*Schizachyrium scoparium*) that are intermixed with various native forb species. The most common introduced terrestrial species are smooth brome (*Bromus inermis*), Kentucky bluegrass (*Poa pratensis*), and crested wheatgrass (*Agropyron cristatum*). These are perennial, sod-forming, cool-season species that are drought resistant. In addition, tall wheatgrass (*Thinopyrum ponticum*), intermediate wheatgrass (*T. intermedium*), pubescent wheatgrass, quackgrass (*Elymus repens*), downy brome (*Bromus tectorum*),

and Japanese brome (*B. japonicus*) occur as scattered inclusions, whereas introduced forbs include sweet clover (*Melilotus* spp.) and alfalfa (*Medicago sativa*). The primary noxious weeds include leafy spurge (*Euphorbia esula*), Canada thistle (*Cirsium arvense*), sow thistle (*Sonchus oleraceus*), and wormwood (*Artemesia* spp.) (BFW).

Management of Huron WMD uplands are primarily directed toward reconstructing grasslands on previously farmed sites and restoring existing grasslands (i.e., native sod with no previous cropping history) that have been invaded by non-native grasses to more native vegetation communities. Reconstruction of previously farmed sites typically begins with cropping for two years to promote a seed bed that is relatively free of weeds. Corn (*Zea mays*) is typically planted in the first year and soybeans (*Glycine max*) in the second year. Soybeans are used in the second year because this crop results in a firm seedbed with little crop residue, which facilitates reseeding native grass the following spring. Approximately three years after an area has been reseeded, some type of management is needed to remove excess dead vegetation and stimulate growth of planted natives. In contrast, grassland restoration efforts attempt to shift the composition of the existing plant community to a higher proportion of native species and do not involve mechanical disturbance of soil and use of crops.

The most common management treatments used in both reconstruction (following initial seeding) and restoration of Huron WMD grasslands are prescribed fire, grazing, or a combination of these strategies (BFW). Prescribed fire was used to treat 2,147 ha (5,305 ac) between 1999 and 2005, whereas grazing and a combination of grazing and fire was implemented on 1,240 ha (3,064 ac) and 1,414 ha (3,494 ac), respectively, between 2000 and 2005 (BFW). The effectiveness of these treatments in stimulating native species and reducing the incidence of non-native species varied depending on location, vegetation community, and time and intensity of treatment.

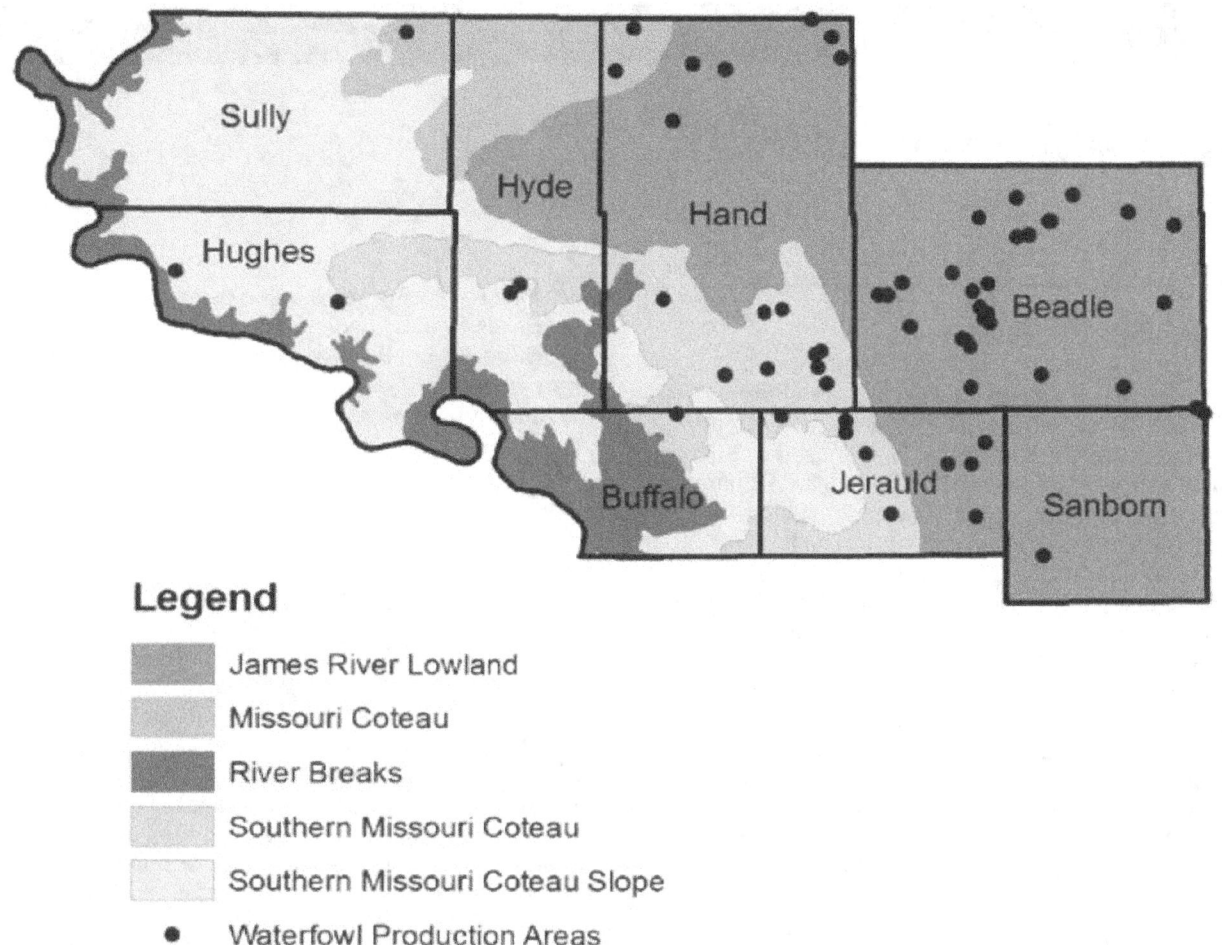

Legend

■	James River Lowland
▨	Missouri Coteau
■	River Breaks
▨	Southern Missouri Coteau
□	Southern Missouri Coteau Slope
●	Waterfowl Production Areas

Figure 1. Level IV ecoregions in the eight-county region of the Huron Wetland Management District, South Dakota (modified from Bryce et al. 1998).

Table 1. Native and non-native species composition of native sod and planted native tracts administered by Huron Wetland Management District, South Dakota, in 2005 (HFW).

	Percent composition of native vegetation									
	<5		5–50		>50–95		>95		Total	
Tract type	Ha (ac)	%	Ha (ac)	%	Ha (ac)	%	Ha (ac)	%	Ha (ac)	
Native sod	1,801	71	600	24	101	4	25	1	2,527	
	(4,450)		(1,507)		(250)		(62)		(6,269)	
Planted natives	135	19	57	8	221	31	300	42	713	
	(334)		(141)		(546)		(744)		(1,762)	

Conceptual Approach

Goal and Objectives

The goal of restoring native grasses and forbs that provide the structure and resources necessary to support target migratory birds was used as guidance in developing the conceptual approach. Although this goal contains general measures of success, ecological restoration is still subject to interpretation because general descriptions of plant community composition (i.e., native grasses and forbs) may not explicitly define expectations of restoration. Approximately 988 species of native vascular plants occur in the tall-grass prairie of the central United States and adjacent Canada (Ladd 1997); however, a given site is not suitable for all of these species. In addition, non-native species dominate many sites designated for restoration and long-term, complete eradication often is not possible (Society of Ecological Restoration 2004). Some tolerance threshold for the non-native species may need to be established, particularly on small restoration projects that are located in highly modified landscapes (D'Antonio and Meyerson 2002, Wilson and Pärtel 2003). Plant species or plant species groups important for providing necessary structure and foods for target bird species should be identified because habitat requirements of these species differ depending on species, annual cycle event, climate, and land-use conditions in the surrounding landscape (Knopf and Samson 1995, Johnson and Igl 2001, Hobbs and Norton 2004). These plant species may not represent the entire complement of desirable species, but they do represent critical community components necessary for success. Consequently, specific species or guilds must be identified to ensure that the target plant community achieves the purposes for which Huron WMD was established. Finally, all metrics that will be used to define success in achieving goals should be explicitly stated. This goal only addresses biological aspects even though political and cultural aspects also must be considered, and often may override biological considerations, when making decisions regarding ecological restoration of some sites.

The existing description of desired condition provides sufficient detail to develop an example framework to evaluate ecological restoration potential. However, if such an approach is used, developing specific objectives that explicitly state desired outcomes will be necessary to make cohesive decisions regarding restoration priorities. Such criteria also will be necessary to design a monitoring program that can be used to periodically assess progress and make sequential decisions regarding the most appropriate strategies to implement.

Spatial Scale

The dynamic attributes of ecosystems, including interactions among organisms and between organisms and their environment, tend to be multi-scaled (Lewis et al. 1996) and this must be considered when evaluating ecological restoration potential and possible strategies. At a large spatial scale, Huron WMD encompasses portions of five Level IV ecoregions (Bryce et al. 1998; Fig. 1). All of these ecoregions are dominated by soils in the Order Mollisol with the exception of the River Breaks, which also includes Aridisols and Entisols. Long-term average annual precipitation and annual growing season days also appear similar among ecoregions, but closer inspection reveals that combinations of these factors result in important differences among ecoregions that are reflected in soil Great Groups (i.e., differentiations within a soil Order based on dominant processes [e.g., drainage]), as well as soil temperature and moisture regimes (Table 2). This information is valuable for evaluating ecological restoration potential because these factors can influence vegetation community composition and structure at larger spatial scales. The James River Lowland and the Missouri Coteau in the north central portion of Huron WMD historically supported vegetation transitional between tall-grass and mixed-grass prairie and dominated by big bluestem, little bluestem, switchgrass, Indiangrass, porcupinegrass, green needlegrass, and prairie junegrass (Koeleria macrantha). In contrast, ecoregions in the western portion of Huron WMD (Southern Missouri Coteau Slope, Southern Missouri Coteau, and River Breaks) exhibit mesic soil temperatures and ustic soil moisture regimes. Historically, vegetation in these ecoregions was dominated by species characteristic of the mixed-grass prairie, including western wheatgrass, green needlegrass, needle-and-thread (*Hesperostipa comata*), little bluestem, and blue grama (*Bouteloua gracilis*). In addition to these grasses, the natural vegetation of the River Breaks also included juniper (*Juniperus* spp.) and deciduous trees on north slopes and draws, as well as cottonwood (*Populus* spp.) gallery forests on the floodplains of the Missouri and James rivers (Gartner and Sieg 1996).

Although broad community descriptions can help establish general restoration guidelines, abiotic and biotic factors also affect plant community establishment, composition, and structure at finer scales. Within a restoration site, differences in soils and climate often occur with subtle changes in topography, slope, and aspect. Such differences can be sufficient to cause shifts in plant community composition and structure across relatively short distances. In many cases, these microsites support vegetation that is not characteristic of the general vegetation community at broader landscape scales. Increasing the success of restoration projects often requires considering this more site-specific information to avoid errors regarding selection of plant species to restore and strategies to implement.

Although a variety of spatial scales could be used to develop an approach for evaluating ecological restoration potential, we decided to use watersheds for Huron WMD lands. Watersheds were selected because evaluation at this scale is the most commonly cited for setting restoration goals (Ehrenfeld 2000). Watersheds are applicable to all lands within Huron WMD regardless of ecoregion, and most lands currently administered by Huron WMD have non-integrated drainage and have a well-defined watershed (i.e., upland area that drains to an isolated wetland) that can be defined using existing spatial data. In addition, abiotic factors (e.g., soils, topography) that affect ecological functions (e.g., nutrient cycling, hydrology) operate at this scale and a watershed approach provides the ability to evaluate functional changes caused by past land-use activities that will be important when developing ecological restoration strategies.

Temporal Scale

Temporal periodicity can significantly influence success of ecological restoration efforts because some factors controlling plant establishment and persistence exhibit considerable variability within and among years. Specific combinations of soil temperature, soil moisture, and photoperiod are often required to break seed dormancy and stimulate seed germination of many species. Climate obviously influences these factors and if all requirements are not met, germination does not occur during that year. Even after initial establishment, these factors continue to play a dominant role in determining annual growth, survival, and reproduction of plants, as well as the species that dominate the plant community.

It is difficult to explicitly incorporate temporal climate variability in an evaluation of restoration potential, but considering a range of values (e.g., quantiles, confidence intervals) for important variables is often more appropriate than using long-term averages. Local or on-site variation in monthly precipitation and temperature can be compared with the germination and growth requirements of plant species when making decisions regarding appropriate seed mixtures to plant on specific sites. Such information,

in combination with the plant species aggregations being established or managed and the life history characteristics of these species, can also be useful for establishing guidelines regarding the proper time to implement various management treatments (e.g., soil disturbance, prescribed fire, grazing). Although the use of this information does not guarantee success, it can help reduce erroneous conclusions during the evaluation process.

Abiotic and Biotic Factors

Establishment of native vegetation suitable to support the habitat requirements of target migratory birds is the primary consideration in the ecological restoration of grasslands on Huron WMD. Most reconstruction projects involve planting of seeds, manipulation of environmental conditions to stimulate germination of seeds already in the seed bank, or a combination of these techniques. In contrast, restoration projects typically occur in native sod (i.e., areas that have never been tilled) and focus on manipulation of existing vegetation communities to promote native grasses and forbs and suppress non-native species. In both cases, understanding processes that control soil propagule bank (e.g., seeds, vegetative propagules) and vegetation dynamics are paramount (Fig. 2). In general, the soil seed bank is comprised of an active and inactive component. Seeds (planted or natural) in the active component are capable of germination and are located in the top 5 cm (2 in) of soil. Seeds in the inactive component are buried deeper than 5 cm (2 in) in the soil profile and cannot germinate because environmental cues stimulating dormancy break and germination are not received. Vegetative propagules (e.g., rhizomes, corms) also exhibit active and inactive components, although the depth of the transition zone tends to occur at greater soil depths. The composition and density of propagules in the active and inactive components constantly change. Propagules already in the soil bank can be moved between the active and inactive component by both natural (e.g., rodents, water) and anthropogenic (e.g., harrowing) factors. In addition, inputs of reproductive structures to the soil bank occur annually as a result of seed production by plants on the site, propagule dispersal (e.g., wind, water, animal) onto the site from nearby areas, and by direct addition of propagules by humans. Propagule loss occurs from both the active and inactive components as a result of pathogens, predation, and physiological or physical death.

Within the active component, only seeds that receive appropriate environmental cues germinate. Primary cues include photoperiod, soil temperature, soil oxygen, soil salinity, and soil moisture (Simpson et al. 1989, Baskin and Baskin 1998, Cronk and Fennessy 2001; Fig. 2). Each of these cues continues to influence survival and reproductive potential following germination (Simpson et al. 1989), but other factors are also important, including nutrient availability, presence of fungal populations, and adaptations to disturbance (Miller 1997, Reynolds et al. 2003, Kulmatiski et al. 2006). Although seemingly simple, the pathways controlling germination, establishment,

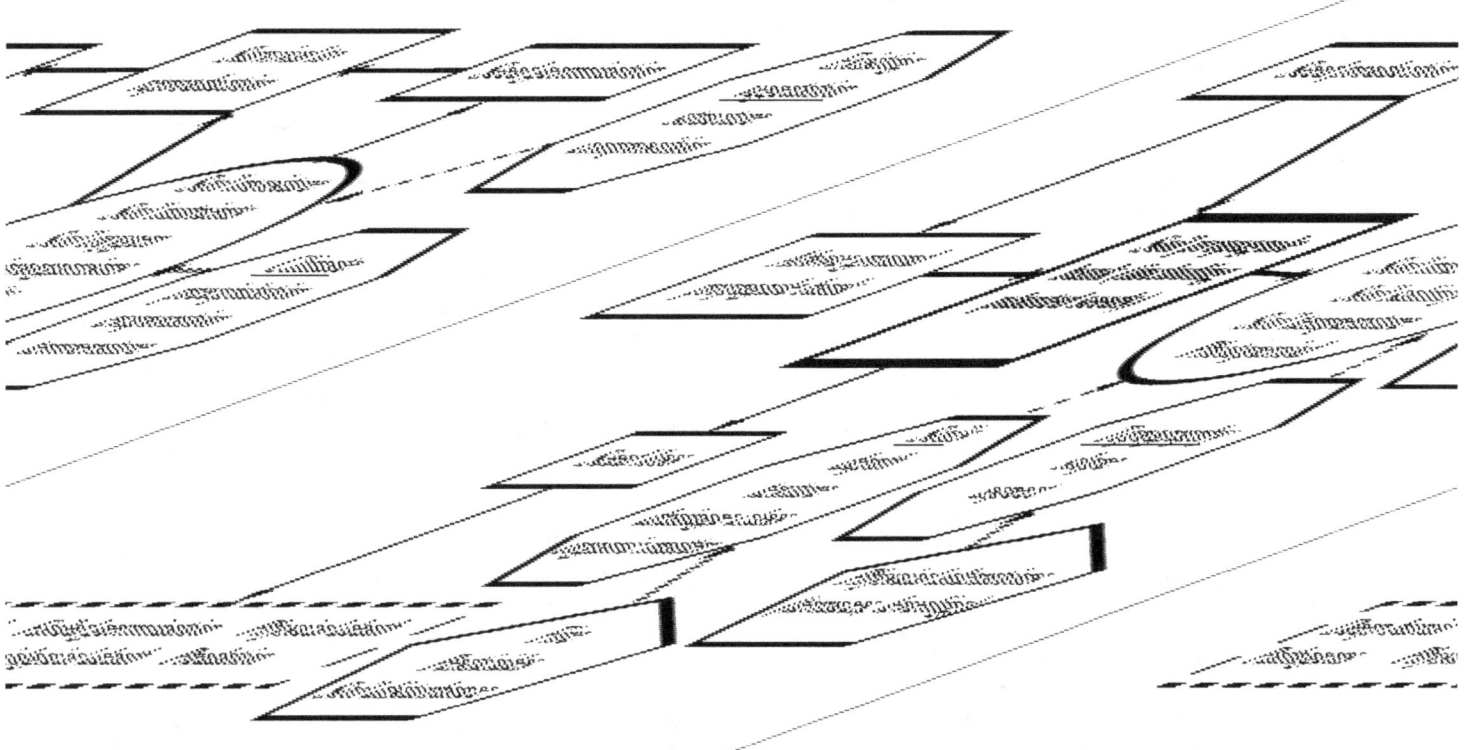

Figure 2. Simplified illustration of seed bank dynamics, including state variables (rectangles), primary abiotic and biotic factors (octagons) influencing plant germination cues and survival (ovals), and common examples of anthropogenic factors influencing abiotic and biotic factors (pentagons). Figure adapted from Simpson et al. 1989.

and survival are extremely complex because many of the environmental factors influencing germination are interrelated; soil temperature tends to increase with increasing photoperiod and soil oxygen content decreases as soil moisture increases. In addition, many germination cues are directly and indirectly influenced by other abiotic and biotic factors (Fig. 2) and the tolerance of individual species to various environmental factors tends to change depending on propagule type (e.g., seed, rhizome) and life history stage (e.g., seedling, adult). Finally, past human activities (e.g., agriculture) have substantially altered interrelationships among the factors that influence the short- and long-term expression of the plant community. Such changes may allow species suited to high resource availability to succeed (Davis et al. 2000, Vinton and Goergen 2006) or disrupt plant-soil feedback mechanisms that affect plant community dynamics, including the invasion potential of exotic species (Calderon et al. 2000, Symstad 2000). The mixing and turning of soil during plowing stimulates the breakdown of soil organic matter and the loss of carbon to the atmosphere (Brye and Pirani 2004). The extent of this loss can be extensive. In North Dakota, soil carbon concentrations in the top 10 cm (4 in) of agricultural soils decreased 33% in 25 years (Bauer and Black 1981). These changes can significantly affect soil depth, texture, and nutrient availability. Tillage also can significantly alter moisture gradients by altering topography and the hydraulic conductivity of soils (Bouma 1991, Messing and Jarvis 1993, Fuentes et al. 2004).

The above discussion focused on the importance of

environmental conditions in assessing site potential relative to plant community germination, establishment, and sustainability. Evaluation of the expected value of the plant community relative to migratory birds is also important given that this was another priority we wanted to consider. Ultimately, the avian response to management should be evaluated directly through pre- and post-project monitoring even though species-habitat relationships often are used to initially evaluate potential responses of target organisms. The most common habitat attributes used to conduct such evaluations are factors related to area (e.g., minimum area required, edge effects, juxtaposition of different habitat types), plant structure, and food production, which in turn are influenced by plant composition. Habitat suitability, as defined by these factors, varies among species and also can change for a single species during different annual cycle events (e.g., breeding, migration, wintering). Given this variability, the most accurate evaluation of potential habitat value for migratory birds requires comparing anticipated site conditions relative to the requirements of multiple species during the appropriate portion of the annual cycle. Criteria for selecting a representative suit of species can be based on numerous considerations, including species mentioned in enabling legislation or species of conservation concern that are provided in various state, regional, and national conservation plans. Given the dynamic nature of grassland plant communities, another consideration is to select species that represent the full range of vegetation conditions that may occur at a site because various attributes, such vegetation structure and types of foods, can differ markedly depending on type of disturbance (e.g., fire, mowing, herbicide application, soil disturbance) and time since the last disturbance occurred. Selecting species that characterize a broad range of plant community composition and structural requirements will help prevent underestimating the avian value of the site. Developing this species list may seem overwhelming, but it is possible to select a pool of relatively few species to represent restoration objectives. While the current number of breeding bird species documented in the Great Plains is approximately 320 (Johnsgard 1979), developing suitable grassland restoration objectives for a local area may focus on as few as 32 bird species to receive priority consideration (Knopf and Samson 1995).

Huron WMD has yet to develop site-specific information on many of the abiotic and biotic factors we identified as important for evaluating ecological restoration potential. Therefore, we conducted a search to identify potential sources of existing information that could be used to evaluate site potential during the interim. With respect to vegetation, we concentrated on selecting factors that influence initial germination and early establishment because most management activities conducted on Huron WMD directly impact these factors. Incorporation of these factors into site evaluations has the potential to help determine the extent of degradation, aid in developing possible remediation measures, and identify appropriate seed mixtures for planting. Many of these factors operate at the watershed scale. In contrast, factors used to evaluate migratory bird benefits focused on defining species-habitat relationships. Although other factors influence bird use, species-habitat relationships can be directly linked to ecological restoration efforts and provide a cohesive method to evaluate potential outcomes with the realization that pre- and post-monitoring of the avian community also is important.

Climate.—Climate variables influencing germination and early establishment include precipitation, evaporation, and ambient temperature, which are primary determinants of soil temperature and soil moisture. Because these factors exhibit high spatial and temporal variability across Huron WMD, site-specific information would be valuable. In the absence of local information, annual and seasonal ranges could be used to evaluate overall site conditions and constraints (High Plains Regional Climate Center 2006, National Climatic Data Center 2006).

Soils.—Important characteristics of soils include the depth, drainage class, texture, and organic matter content of soil horizons (Nelson and Anderson 1983). Drainage class (e.g., well drained, moderately well drained, very poorly drained) provides a measure of the residency time of soil water, whereas texture and organic matter content provides a measure of the moisture and nutrient retention capacity of soils (Fig. 2). In general, soils high in sand tend to retain water for only a short period and have lower nutrient concentrations and moisture concentrations than soils higher in clay and silt. Collectively, these soil properties influence key factors

that control germination and early establishment of plant species. Abrupt discontinuities in species distributions can often be explained by differences in soil depth and texture (Nelson and Anderson 1983). General soil attribute data can be obtained from county soil maps and in both tabular and spatial forms (U.S. Department Agriculture 2006).

Topography.—Slope and aspect are among the most important topographic variables because they influence soil moisture and temperature (Kline 1997). In general, slope influences soil moisture gradients, whereas aspect influences the time and extent of soil exposure to drying winds and sunlight. Steeper slopes tend to exhibit steeper soil moisture gradients over a smaller area, with low elevations typically being the wettest and higher elevations being driest. Within this context, south slopes tend to be the hottest and north slopes tend to be the coolest. Collectively, these factors can result in diverse environmental niches within a watershed that support distinct vegetation communities. For example, changes in species composition that occur with gradual elevation shifts often are due to moisture gradients (Dix and Smeins 1967, Clambey and Landers 1978). General information on slope and aspect often can be determined from a combination of aerial photographs, digital elevation models, topography data, or other remotely sensed data (U.S. Geological Survey 2006). Depending on resolution and data type, subtle differences in topography may not be detected and field reconnaissance may be required. Equipment necessary to development site-specific information is readily available and time requirements are minimal to moderate. Additional advantages of on-site reconnaissance include ground-truthing soils information and documenting plant species composition and distribution.

Vegetation.—Information on climate, soils, and topography must be considered in the context of plant ecology to be useful in evaluating restoration potential. Important plant information includes a list of plant species grouped into functional guilds that currently or historically occupied sites being considered for restoration, knowledge of factors that control germination, establishment, and survival of plants in each functional guild, and physical traits of plants that provide wildlife value. Functional groups can be defined using several different classification methods (e.g., life form, growth form, metabolic pathway) alone or in combination. The most commonly used categories include annual/perennial, grass/forb, and cool-season/ warm-season, but other combinations can be developed depending on restoration goals.

Relative to plant germination and establishment, the most important factors include type of seed dormancy (e.g., none, physical, physiological) and environmental conditions required to break seed dormancy (e.g., scarification, cold stratification) and stimulate germination (Simpson et al. 1989, Baskin and Baskin 1998, Cronk and Fennessy 2001; Fig. 2). In addition to these factors, nutrient and moisture requirements, as well as disturbance tolerance are important for

determining plant survival (Miller 1997, Reynolds et al. 2003, Kulmatiski et al. 2006). Physical traits that often are important for determining wildlife value include growth form, plant height, and food production potential (Laubhan et al. 2006).

Collectively, information on the ecology of individual plant species can serve several useful purposes. Species autecology is important in determining appropriate species to plant (reconstruction) and designing management treatments (reconstruction and restoration) (Simberloff 1990, Vitousek 1990). Seed mixtures comprised of more drought-tolerant species may be more applicable in semi-arid areas (e.g., south-facing hillslopes), whereas a greater complement of mesic species may be more appropriate near drainages where soil temperatures are cooler and moisture is more available. From a management treatment perspective, application of fire or grazing should be timed to match the appropriate growth stage or annual cycle event of plants species being managed. This information can be used to time treatments to more effectively control undesirable plants (e.g., treatment applied when plant species is most vulnerable to stress) or, conversely, to stimulate desirable species (e.g., treatment applied to increase sunlight penetration and moisture during initiation of growth in spring). Knowledge of historic and/or current native plant distributions also helps define potential species composition at different times during the restoration process (Palmer et al. 1997) and can be useful in evaluating project success. For example, application of a management treatment or seed mixture to stimulate certain desirable species may not

result in the expected response. In general, this could occur due to inappropriate timing of a management treatment or planting an inappropriate seed mixture. Conversely, the lack of response could be caused by environmental conditions that are outside human control. Differentiating between these causes is difficult, but understanding plant germination and growth requirements can help prevent drawing inappropriate conclusions. In addition, the species or functional species groups currently or recently occupying the restoration site can provide insight to environmental conditions that may influence plant germination and establishment (Bever 1994, Reynolds et al. 2003), or indicate potential changes in ecological processes or abiotic factors that have occurred due to past land use activities (Kulmatiski et al. 2006). For example, the presence of drought-tolerant species near a stream course could indicate a change in soil properties or a disruption in the soil moisture gradient.

Numerous approaches can be used to develop lists of current and historic plant species. The vegetation distribution map and plant community inventory produced by Huron WMD are ideal sources for developing a list of current plant species, whereas species comprising historic communities can be obtained from various geographic databases, publications, and surveys (e.g., General Land Office, railroad rights-of-way). The list of historic species does not need to be exhaustive because some species may compensate functionally for other species (Naeem et al. 1994, Tilman et al. 1994, Kindscher and Wells 1995, Piper 1995, Tilman 1996), but this list should include annuals, perennials, and keystone species that are functionally important. Mutualistic relationships exist between some animals (e.g., pollinators) and plant species (Ries and Debinski 2001, Travers et al. 2011) or certain plant species may be involved in the regulation of nutrients important during initial establishment (Miller 1997). Following compilation of the plant species list, information on plant germination and growth requirements of these species can be located in electronic databases, reputable websites and seed catalogues, books, dissertations, and scientific journals. In many cases, information on all important factors will not be available for a given plant species. This is not problematic because individual species can be grouped into functional guilds.

Wildlife.--Habitat requirements vary depending on the species and the annual cycle events that occur on the site, but area requirements, nest site characteristics, foraging site conditions, and foods are important factors in determining habitat quality for many avian species.

Information on habitat requirements can be obtained from numerous sources, including electronic databases, literature syntheses, and scientific journals (Laubhan et al. 2006), but the quality of data should be evaluated relative to the intended purpose of use. Qualitative information (e.g., tall, dense) is difficult to use in evaluating habitat suitability because it only provides a general impression of required conditions. In contrast, quantitative measures (e.g., range, confidence intervals) are more valuable because they can be compared directly to vegetation measures collected on the site. In addition, care should be exercised when interpreting off-site information because habitat requirements reported from different geographic areas may or may not be directly applicable to sites on Huron WMD due to differences in climate, plant composition, landscape conditions, or other factors (Bakker et al. 2002, Laubhan et al. 2008).

Framework Development

Historically, the development of ecological restoration strategies largely has been based on knowledge gained from experiments to restore degraded landscapes (King and Hobbs 2006). These strategies may or may not be successful when applied to sites that differ with respect to various abiotic and biotic factors, which suggests that formulation of a sound restoration approach requires more than anecdotal information (Hobbs and Norton 1996, Choi 2004). Further, increasing the chance of project success relative to desired goals requires not only the capability to implement various techniques (e.g., seed source, equipment), but also developing an understanding of when different techniques are most applicable.

To address the considerations described above, numerous approaches have been developed to evaluate a site and determine the most appropriate restoration strategy. One approach is to use reference sites (Society of Ecological Restoration 2004). Comparison of environmental conditions at the reference site and degraded site can provide valuable insight that can be used to develop realistic goals and identify possible restoration scenarios. Unfortunately, the utility of reference sites is sometimes limited because they are difficult to identify and the structure and function of these areas may not be known (Michener 1997, White and Walker 1997). Another approach, which is used in this report, is to develop a decision analysis model or schema that focuses on key attributes considered critical to restoring structure and function (Aronson et al. 1993, Milton et al. 1994, Box 1996, Ludwig et al. 1997, Perrow and Davy 2002, Temperton et al. 2004). Applicability of such models in a field setting requires time- and cost-efficient collection of relevant information. In the previous section, ideas were provided on sources of data for potentially important factors that are already available and either free or relatively inexpensive to acquire. In some cases, this information may not be of sufficient quality and more costly methods of acquiring necessary data may be necessary.

The framework developed for evaluating restoration potential on Huron WMD lands is comprised of goals, objectives, attributes, and outcomes (Fig. 3). The goal represents the purpose of constructing the decision model and objectives describe in more detail what values will be considered when determining priorities. Attributes represent the primary factors identified in the previous section that are used to

© Chris Bailey

assess site conditions relative to the objectives and interim steps (ovals) are examples of how attribute information can be combined to facilitate evaluation. Outcomes (represented by the double boxes in Fig. 3) are based on evaluation of the attributes and could be used to assign priorities to restoration projects.

Huron WMD will establish grassland goals and objectives during the CCP process that may differ somewhat from the general description used in this report. As an example, we developed a conceptual schema based on the goal of evaluating the reconstruction potential of individual WPAs in Huron WMD. Obviously, there are numerous other objectives (e.g., developing appropriate management strategies for restoring native sod communities) and attributes that could be included to provide a more thorough evaluation. Given that on-site data regarding additional attributes on Huron WMD lands currently is limited and management decisions cannot be postponed until this data is collected,

Figure 3. A conceptual approach for evaluating restoration potential of grasslands.

we developed our approach based on available information to assist Huron WMD in the decision process.

Example objectives were designated as developing appropriate seed mixtures for reconstruction projects that benefit migratory birds, estimating the potential for non-native plant species establishment, and determining wildlife values that would be expected following restoration. To accomplish the evaluation, attributes were grouped into three categories (abiotic, land-use history, and biotic) to aid interpretation. The abiotic attributes include topographic and soils data from the watershed encompassing the site. In this example, the topographic and soils data would be intersected using a geographic information system to delineate unique combinations of soils, slopes, and aspects. In addition, information on altered soil structure and/or hydrology caused by past land-use activities could be incorporated into this matrix (Fig. 3). Field examination could reveal that tillage has caused the loss of soil organic matter or aerial photography could identify the presence of terraces that have interrupted the soil moisture gradient along a slope. This information could be used to delineate and map zones with unique abiotic properties in the restoration site that could influence plant species composition, ease of establishment, and areas where more intensive management may be required. Topographically low, poorly drained alluvial soils (typically rich in organic matter) that would support plants requiring increased soil moisture could be separated from adjacent toe-slopes with rapid drainage (typically moderate amounts of organic matter) that would support more xeric species. The environmental characteristics of each zone could then be compared with the germination/reproductive requirements of available plant species in the various functional groups to help determine appropriate seed mixtures for each zone. The value (or priority) of restoring the site could be determined by comparing current wildlife values with anticipated post-restoration values based on differences in the amount of contiguous grassland area provided, plant structure, and food resources that would occur if restoration is successful.

Conclusions

Developing an approach for evaluating and prioritizing sites for restoration is a complex and uncertain process. Although much is known regarding factors controlling plant community establishment and relationships between plant communities and wildlife habitat suitability, the relative importance of these factors often varies among and within sites depending on past perturbations and surrounding landscape conditions. Detailed information regarding many of these factors often is limited on specific sites and intra- and inter-annual climate variability make it impossible to accurately predict future environmental conditions. Therefore, it is not possible to develop a single restoration strategy that is appropriate for all sites, or even all landscape conditions within a site, and even management treatments that are appropriately tailored to a site may not yield expected results. Given this uncertainty, general schemas that incorporate abiotic and biotic factors related to the dynamic processes influencing plant community composition and structure must be developed to guide restoration.

The conceptual framework we developed is intended to serve this purpose, but additional work must be accomplished before this model could be implemented because the objectives used in the model are examples developed by the authors and the attributes selected for inclusion are based on a review of the literature rather than field data collected on Huron WMD. Hopefully, Huron WMD will continue to develop this approach because a conceptual framework assists in the identification of attributes important in evaluating outcomes. Most individuals recognize the impact of abiotic factors and past land use in determining plant community composition and structure, but this contributes little to developing management approaches if specific factors and their relationship to achieving goals are not defined. A structured framework also promotes standardized evaluations and can improve communication as it provides a method to systematically deconstruct complex problems and provide greater objectivity when making restoration decisions (Cipollini et al. 2005). Finally, frameworks that incorporate abiotic and biotic factors as primary determinants of expected outcomes can facilitate implementing an adaptive management process (Walters and Holling 1990, Haney and Power 1996).

Literature Cited

Aronson, J., and E. Le Floc'h. 1996. Vital landscape attributes: missing tools for restoration ecology. Restoration Ecology 4:327-333.

Aronson, J., C. Floret, E. Le Floc'h, C. Ovalle, and R. Pontanier. 1993. Restoration and rehabilitation of degraded ecosystems in arid and semi-arid lands. I. A view from the south. Restoration Ecology 1:8-17.

Bakker, K. K., D. E. Naugle, and K. F. Higgins. 2002. Incorporating landscape attributes into models for migratory grassland bird conservation. Conservation Biology 16:1638-1646.

Baskin, C. C., and J. M. Baskin. 1998. Seeds: ecology, biogeography, and evolution of dormancy and germination. Academic Press, New York.

Bauer, A., and A. L. Black. 1981. Soil carbon, nitrogen, and bulk density comparisons in two cropland tillage systems after 25 years and in virgin grassland. Soil Science Society of America Journal 45:1166-1170.

Bever, J. D. 1994. Feedback between plants and their soil communities in an old field community. Ecology 75:1965-1977.

Bouma, J. 1991. Influence of soil macroporosity on environmental quality. Agronomy 46:1-37.

Box, J. 1996. Setting objectives and defining outputs for ecological restoration and habitat creation. Restoration Ecology 4:427-432.

Breshears, D. D., J. A. Ludwig, S. N. Martens, P. C. Beeson, B. P. Wilcox, and C. D. Allen. 2001. Runoff and erosion thresholds: implications for rangeland degradation and restoration. Ecological Society of America Annual Meeting Abstracts 86:8-9.

Bryce, S., J. M. Omernik, D. E. Pater, M. Ulmer, J. Schaar, J. Freeouf, R. Johnson, P. Kuck, and S. H. Azevedo [Online]. 1998. Ecoregions of North Dakota and South Dakota. Northern Prairie Wildlife Research Center, Jamestown, North Dakota. <http://www.npwrc.usgs.gov/resource/1998/ndsdeco/ndsdeco.htm> (31 October 2006).

Brye, K. R., and A. L. Pirani. 2004. Native soil quality and the effects of tillage in the Grand Prairie Region of eastern Arkansas. American Midland Naturalist 154:28-41.

Buckley, G. P., editor. 1989. Biological habitat reconstruction. Belhaven Press, London, United Kingdom.

Byre, V. J. 1997. Birds. Pages 327-337 *in* S. Packard and C. F. Mutel, editors. The tallgrass restoration handbook for prairies, savannas, and woodlands. Island Press, New York.

Cairns, J., Jr. 1991. The status of the theoretical and applied science of restoration ecology. Environmental Professional 13:1-9.

Calderon, F. J., L. E. Jackson, K. M. Scow, and D. E. Rolston. 2000. Microbial responses to simulated tillage in cultivated and uncultivated soils. Soil Biology and Biochemistry 32:1547-1559.

Choi, Y. D. 2004. Theories for ecological restoration in changing environments: toward 'futuristic' restoration. Ecological Research 19:75-81.

Cipollini, K. A., A. L. Maruyama, and C. L. Zimmerman. 2005. Planning for restoration: a decision analysis approach to prioritization. Restoration Ecology 13:460-470.

Clambey, G. K., and R. Q. Landers. 1978. A survey of wetland vegetation in north-central Iowa. Pages 32-35 *in* D. C. Glenn-Lewin and R. Q. Landers, Jr., editors. Proceedings of the 5th Midwest Prairie Conference, Ames, Iowa.

Cronk, J. K., and M. S. Fennessy. 2001. Wetland plants: biology and ecology. Lewis Publishers, New York.

D'Antonio, C., and L. A. Meyerson. 2002. Exotic plant species as problems and solutions in ecological restoration: a synthesis. Restoration Ecology 10:703-713.

Davis, G. W., and D. M. Richardson. 1995. Mediterranean-type ecosystems: the function of biodiversity. Springer-Verlag, Berlin, Germany.

Davis, M. A., J. P. Grime, and K. Thompson. 2000. Fluctuating resources in plant communities: a general theory of invasibility. Journal of Ecology 88:528-534.

Dix, R. L., and F. E. Smeins. 1967. The prairie, meadow, and marsh vegetation of Nelson County, North Dakota. Canadian Journal of Botany 45:21-58.

Ehrenfeld, J. G. 2000. Defining the limits of restoration: the need for realistic goals. Restoration Ecology 8:2-9.

Eliason, S. A., and E. B. Allen. 1997. Exotic grass competition in suppressing native shrubland re-establishment. Restoration Ecology 5:245-255.

Falk, D. A., C. I. Millar, and M. Olwell, editors. 1996. Restoring diversity: strategies for the reintroduction of endangered plants. Island Press, Washington, D.C.

Friedel, M. H. 1991. Range condition assessment and the concept of thresholds: a viewpoint. Journal of Range Management 44:422-426.

Fuentes, J. P., M. Flury, and D. F. Bezdicek. 2004. Hydraulic properties in a silt loam soil under natural prairie, conventional till, and no till. Soil Science Society of America Journal 68:1679-1688.

Gartner, F. R., and C. H. Sieg. 1996. South Dakota rangelands: more than a sea of grass. Rangelands 18:212-216.

George, T. L., and S. Zack. 2001. Spatial and temporal considerations in restoring habitat for wildlife. Restoration Ecology 9:272-279.

Goldstein, P. Z. 1999. Functional ecosystems and biodiversity buzzwords. Conservation Biology 13:247-255.

Haney, A., and R. L. Power. 1996. Adaptive management for sound ecosystem management. Environmental Management 20:879-886.

Higgs, E. S. 1997. What is good ecological restoration? Conservation Biology 11:338-348.

High Plains Regional Climate Center [Online]. 2006. Current climate summary maps. <http://www.hprcc.unl.edu> (24 May 2012).

Hobbs, R. J., and D. A. Norton. 2004. Ecological filters, thresholds, and gradients in resistance to ecosystem reassembly. Pages 72-95 in V. M. Temperton, R. J. Hobbs, T. Nuttle, and S. Halle, editors. Assembly rules and restoration ecology. Island Press, Washington, D.C.

Hobbs, R. J., and D. A. Norton. 1996. Towards a conceptual framework for restoration ecology. Restoration Ecology 4:93-110.

Holling, C. S. 1973. Resilience and stability of ecological systems. Annual Review of Ecology and Systematics 4:1-23.

Horne, J. K., and D. C. Schneider. 1995. Spatial variance in ecology. Oikos 74:18-26.

Jarrell, W. M., and R. A. Virginia. 1990. Soil cation accumulation in a mesquite woodland: sustained production and long-term estimates of water use and nitrogen fixation. Journal of Arid Environments 18:51-56.

Jenkins, M. B., R. A. Virginia, and W. M. Jarrell. 1987. Rhizobial ecology of the woody legume mesquite (Prosopis glandulosa) in a Sonoran Desert arroyo. Plant and Soil 105:113-120.

Johnsgard, P. A. 1979. Birds of the Great Plains. University of Nebraska Press, Lincoln, Nebraska.

Johnson, D. H., and L. D. Igl. 2001. Area requirements of grassland birds: a regional perspective. Auk 188:24-34.

Jordan, W. R., M. E. Gilpin, and J. D. Aber, editors. 1987. Restoration ecology: a synthetic approach to ecological research. Cambridge University Press, Cambridge, United Kingdom.

Keddy, P. 1999. Wetland restoration: the potential for assembly rules in the service of conservation. Wetland 19:716-732.

Kershner, J. L. 1997. Setting riparian/aquatic objectives within a watershed context. Restoration Ecology 5:15-24.

Kindscher, K., and P. V. Wells. 1995. Prairie plant guilds: a multivariate analysis of prairie species based on ecological and morphological traits. Vegetatio 117:29-50.

King, E. G., and R. J. Hobbs. 2006. Identifying linkages among conceptual models of ecosystem degradation and restoration: towards an integrative framework. Restoration Ecology 14:369-378.

Kline, V. M. 1997. Planning a restoration. Pages 31-46 in S. Packard and C. F. Mutel, editors. The tallgrass restoration handbook for prairies, savannas, and woodlands. Island Press, New York.

Knopf, F. L. and F. B. Samson. 1995. Conserving the biotic integrity of the Great Plains. Pages 121-133 in S. R. Johnson and A. Bouzaher, editors. Conservation of Great Plains ecosystems: current science, future options. Kluwer Academic Publishers, Dordrecht, The Netherlands.

Kulmatiski, A. K. H. Beard, and J. M. Stark. 2006. Soil history as a primary control on plant invasion in abandoned agricultural fields. Journal of Applied Ecology 43:8868-876.

Ladd, D. 1997. Appendix A: Vascular plants of midwestern tallgrass prairies. Pages 351-355 in S. Packard and C. F. Mutel, editors. The tallgrass restoration handbook for prairies, savannas, and woodlands. Island Press, New York.

Laubhan, M. K., K. E. Kermes, and R. A. Gleason. 2008. Proposed approach to assess potential wildlife habitat suitability on program lands. Pages 45-58 *in* R. A. Gleason, M. K. Laubhan, and N. H. Euliss, Jr., editors. Ecosystem services derived from wetland conservation practices in the United States Prairie Pothole Region with an emphasis on the U.S. Department of Agriculture Conservation Reserve and Wetland Reserve Programs. U.S. Department of the Interior, U.S. Geological Survey Professional Paper 1745.

Laubhan, M. K., R. A. Gleason, N. H. Euliss, Jr., G. A. Knutsen, and R. A. Laubhan. 2006. A preliminary biological assessment of Long Lake National Wildlife Refuge Complex, North Dakota, USA. U.S. Department of Interior, Fish and Wildlife Service, Biological Technical Publication FWS/BTP R6006-2006, Washington, D.C.

Laylock, W. A. 1991. Stable states and thresholds of range condition on North American rangelands: a viewpoint. Journal of Range Management 44:427-433.

Lewis, C. A., N. P. Lester, A. D. Bradshaw, J. E. Fitzgibbon, K. Fuller, L. Hakanson, and C. Richards. 1996. Considerations of scale in habitat conservation and restoration. Canadian Journal of Fisheries and Aquatic Sciences 53(S1):440-445.

Lockwood, J. L., and S. L. Pimm. 1999. When does restoration succeed? Pages 363-392 *in* E. Weiher and P. Keddy, editors. Ecological assembly rules. Cambridge University Press, Cambridge, United Kingdom.

Ludwig, J. A., D. J. Tongway, D. Freudenberger, J. Noble, and K. Hodgkinson, editors. 1997. Landscape ecology, function and management: principles from Australia's rangelands. CSIRO Publishing, Melbourne, Australia.

Messing, I., and N. J. Jarvis. 1993. Temporal variation in the hydraulic conductivity of a tilled clay soil as measured by tension infiltrometers. Journal of Soil Science 44:11-24.

Michener, W. K. 1997. Quantitatively evaluating restoration "experiments": research design, statistical analysis, and data management considerations. Restoration Ecology 5:324-337.

Miller, R. M. 1997. Prairie underground. Pages 23-27 *in* S. Packard and C. F. Mutel, editors. The tallgrass restoration handbook for prairies, savannas, and woodlands. Island Press, New York.

Milton, S. J., W. R. J. Dean, M. A. Du Plessis, and W. R. Siegfried. 1994. A conceptual model of arid rangeland degradation: the escalating cost of declining productivity. Bioscience 44:70-76.

Montalvo, A. M., S. L. Williams, K. J. Rice, S. L. Buchmann, C. Cory, S. N. Handel, G. P. Nabhan, R. Primack, and R. H. Robichaux. 1997. Restoration biology: a population biology perspective. Restoration Ecology 5:277-290.

Naeem, S., L. J. Thompson, S. P. Lawler, J. H. Lawton, and R. M. Woodfin. 1994. Declining biodiversity can alter the performance of ecosystems. Nature 368:734-737.

National Climatic Data Center [Online]. 2006. Monthly surface data. National Oceanic and Atmospheric Administration, Asheville, North Carolina. <http://www.ncdc.noaa.gov/oa/ncdc.html> (24 May 2012).

Nelson, D. C., and R. C. Anderson. 1983. Factors related to the distribution of prairie plants along a moisture gradient. American Midland Naturalist 109:367-375.

Paine, R. T. 1966. Food web complexity and species diversity. American Naturalist 100:65-75.

Palmer, M. A., and N. L. Poff. 1997. The influence of environmental heterogeneity on patterns and processes in streams. Journal of the North American Benthological Society 16:169-173.

Palmer, M. A., R. F. Ambrose, and N. L. Poff. 1997. Ecological theory and community restoration ecology. Restoration Ecology 5:291-300.

Perrow, M. R., and A. J. Davy, editors. 2002. Handbook of ecological restoration. Volume 1. Principals of restoration. Cambridge University Press, Cambridge, United Kingdom.

Pickett, S. T. A., and V. T. Parker. 1994. Avoiding the old pitfalls: opportunities in a new discipline. Restoration Ecology 2:75-79.

Pickett, S.T.A., V. T. Parker, and P. G. Fiedler. 1992. The new paradigm in ecology: implications for conservation biology above the species level. Pages 66-88 *in* P. L. Fiedler and S. K. Sain, editors. Conservation biology. Chapman and Hall, New York.

Piper, J. K. 1995. Composition of prairie plant communities on productive versus unproductive sites in wet and dry years. Canadian Journal of Botany 73:1635-1644.

Piper, J. K., and S. L. Pimm. 2002. The creation of diverse prairie-like communities. Community Ecology 3:205-216.

Reynolds, H. L., A. Packer, J. D. Bever, and K. Clay. 2003. Grassroots ecology: plant-microbe-soil interactions of plant community structure and dynamics. Ecology 84:2281-2291.

Ries, L., and D. M. Debinski. 2001. Butterfly responses to habitat edges in the highly fragmented prairies of Central Iowa. Journal of Animal Ecology 70:840-852.

Risser, P. G. 1995. Biodiversity and ecosystem function. Conservation Biology 9:742-746.

Ruiz-Jaen, M. C., and T. M. Aide. 2005. Restoration success: how is it being measured? Restoration Ecology 13:569-577.

Schulze, E.-D., and H. A. Mooney. 1993. Biodiversity and ecosystem function. Springer-Verlag, Berlin, Germany.

Sheley, R. L., and J. Krueger-Mangold. 2003. Principles for restoring invasive plant-infested rangeland. Weed Science 51:260-265.

Simberloff, D. 1990. Community effects of biological introductions and their implications for restoration. Pages 128-136 *in* D. R. Towns, C. H. Daugherty, and I. A. Atkinson, editors. Engineered organisms in the environment: scientific issues. American Society for Microbiology, Washington, D.C.

Simpson, R. L., M. A. Leck, and V. T. Parker. 1989. Seed banks: general concepts and methodological issues. Pages 3-21 *in* M. A. Leck, V. T. Parker, and R. L. Simpson, editors. Ecology of soil seed banks. Academic Press, San Diego, California.

Society for Ecological Restoration International Science and Policy Working Group (SER). 2004. The SER international primer on ecological restoration. Society for Ecological Restoration International, Tucson, Arizona. <http://www.ser.org/> (31 October 2006).

Symstad, A. J. 2000. A test of the effects of functional group richness and composition on grassland invisibility. Ecology 81:99-109.

Temperton, V. M., R. J. Hobbs, T. Nuttle, and S. Halle, editors. 2004. Assembly rules and restoration ecology: bridging the gap between theory and practice. Island Press, Washington, D.C.

Tilman, D. 1996. Biodiversity: population versus ecosystem stability. Ecology 77:350-363.

Tilman, D. J., A. Downing, and D. A. Wedin. 1994. Does diversity beget stability? Nature 371:257-264.

Tongway, D. J., and J. A. Ludwig. 1996. Rehabilitation of semiarid landscapes in Autralia. I. Restoring productive soil patches. Restoration Ecology 4:388-397.

Travers, S. E., G. M. Fauske, K. Fox, A. A. Ross, and M. O. Harris. 2011. The hidden benefits of pollinator diversity for rangelands of the Great Plains: western prairie fringed orchids as a case study. Rangelands 33:20-26.

U.S. Department of Agriculture [Online]. 2006. Soil attribute data. U.S. Department of Agriculture, Natural Resources Conservation Service. <http://soildatamart.nrcs.usda.gov> (24 May 2012).

U.S. Fish and Wildlife Service. 2000. South Dakota briefing book. Unpublished report. U.S. Department of Interior, Fish and Wildlife Service. <http://moutain-prairie.fws.gov/reference/> (31 October 2006).

U.S. Geological Survey [Online]. 2006. National geospatial program. U.S. Department of Interior, Geological Survey. <http://www.usgs.gov/ngpo> (24 May 2012).

Vitousek, P. M. 1990. Biological invasions and ecosystem processes: towards an integration of population biology and ecosystem studies. Oikos 57:7-13.

Vinton, M. A., and E. M. Goergen. 2006. Plant-soil feedbacks contribute to the persistence of *Bromus inermis* in Tallgrass Prairie. Ecosystems 9:967-976.

Walters, C. J., and C. S. Holling. 1990. Large-scale managements and learning by doing. Ecology 71:2060-2068.

Whisenant, S. G. 1995. Landscape dynamics and arid land restoration. Pages 26-34 *in* B. A. Roundy, E. McArthur, E. Durant, J. S. Haley, and D. K. Mann, compilers. Proceedings: wildland shrub and arid land restoration symposium. U.S. Department of Agriculture Forest Service General Technical Report INT-GTR-315, Ogden, Utah.

Whisenant, S. G. 1999. Repairing damaged wildlands: a process-oriented, landscape-scale approach. Cambridge University Press, Cambridge, United Kingdom.

White, P. S., and J. L. Walker 1997. Approximating nature's variation: selecting and using reference sites and reference information in restoration ecology. Restoration Ecology 5:338-349.

Wiens, J. A. 1984. On understanding a non-equilibrium world: myth and reality in community patterns and processes. Pages 439-457 *in* D. R. Strong, D. Simberloff, L. G. Abele, and A. G. Thistle, editors. Ecological communities: conceptual issues and the evidence. Princeton University Press, Princeton, New Jersey.

Wilson, S. D., and M. Pärtel. 2003. Extirpation or coexistence? Management of a persistent introduced grass in a prairie restoration. Restoration Ecology 11:410-416.

Wissel, C. 1984. A universal law of the characteristic return time near thresholds. Oecologia 65:101-107.